30687

Who Was
Wolfgang Amadeus
Mozart?

Who Was Wolfgang Amadeus Mozart?

By Yona Zeldis McDonough
Illustrated by Carrie Robbins

Grosset & Dunlap • New York

For my children, James and Katherine
McDonough—Y.Z.M.

To Richard, who may not have the chance to see the
finished book, but whose spirit is in
every picture. With love always—C.R.

Text copyright © 2003 by Yona Zeldis McDonough. Illustrations copyright © 2003 by Carrie
Robbins. Cover illustration copyright © 2003 by Nancy Harrison. All rights reserved. Published by
Grosset & Dunlap, a division of Penguin Putnam Books for Young Readers, 345 Hudson Street,
New York, NY 10014. GROSSET & DUNLAP is a trademark of Penguin Putnam Inc. Published
simultaneously in Canada. Printed in the U.S.A.

Library of Congress Cataloging-in-Publication Data

McDonough, Yona Zeldis.
  Who was Wolfgang Amadeus Mozart? / by Yona Zeldis McDonough ;
illustrated by Carrie Robbins.
    p. cm.
Summary: Explores the life and work of the prolific eighteenth-century
Austrian composer who began life as a child prodigy, composing music at
the age of five, and died a pauper at age thirty-five.
1. Mozart, Wolfgang Amadeus, 1756-1791—Juvenile literature.
2. Composers—Austria—Biography—Juvenile literature. [1. Mozart, Wolfgang
Amadeus, 1756-1791. 2. Composers.] I. Title.
ML3930.M9 M21 2003
780'.92—dc21

                                        2002151261

ISBN 0-448-43104-1 (pbk)   A B C D E F G H I J
ISBN 0-448-43154-8 (GB)   A B C D E F G H I J

Contents

Contents

Who Was
Wolfgang Amadeus Mozart?

More than 200 years ago, there was a little boy who learned to play a musical instrument at the age of three. It was called a clavier, which was an old-fashioned stringed instrument that also had a keyboard. By the time he was five, he was composing beautiful music—all by himself. At eight, he had learned to play two more instruments, the violin and the organ. Now he could play three instruments.

1

His father was a musician, too. He wanted everyone to pay attention to his talented son. But some people had a hard time believing that a small boy could be so talented. They thought his father had written the music for him. Or that the boy wasn't a child at all, but a very small adult. There had to be some kind of trick.

A man who was both a lawyer and a musician decided to find out. He tested the boy for many hours. He asked the boy to play a very difficult piece of music. The boy played it easily and well. Then he asked the boy to make up a piece of music for him, right there on the spot. Again, the boy did an excellent job.

Then, a cat came into the room. Right away, the boy stopped playing music and got up to chase it. There was no doubt in the man's mind. The boy was really just a boy, except when he played or wrote music. Then the boy was a genius.

Who was this boy? His name was Wolfgang Amadeus Mozart, and here is his story.

Wolfgang Amadeus Mozart

Chapter 1
Little Boy, Big Talent

Leopold Mozart

Papa Leopold Mozart was very strict. He was a composer and violinist in Salzburg in Austria. When he was finished working for the day, Leopold came home and gave his daughter and son music lessons. Over and over they played what he taught them. They spent hours every day practicing. Both children became really good musicians. But the boy, Wolfgang, was even more talented than his sister.

Wolfgang was born on January 27, 1756, in Salzburg, Austria. (On the map, the little star inside the Austrian monarchy shows where Salzburg is.) Six children had come before him, so he was the baby of the family. But only Wolfgang and his big sister, Maria Anna, lived past their first birthdays. Back then, when babies or young children got sick, there were no medicines like there are today. So, sadly, it was common for children to die.

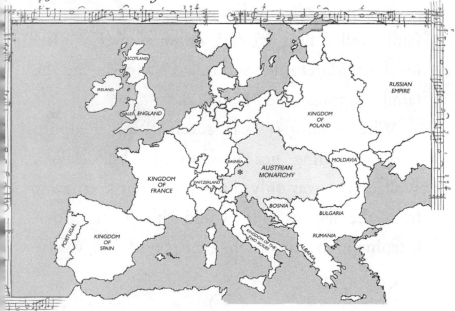

Europe, mid-18th century

Because Wolfgang had such a long name, his family called him Wolferl, or sometimes Wolfie, for short. Maria Anna was called Nannerl. And the family dog was called Bumperl.

When Nannerl was seven, Papa Leopold started teaching her how to play the clavier. Wolfie, who was only three, could not keep away from the lessons. He would sit on the floor, listening to the music while she played. But Wolfie was not satisfied. He wanted more: He wanted to play, too. After Nannerl's lesson was over, he went up to the clavier. He was so small that he had to stand on his toes to reach the keys. He tried one note and then another. He liked the sounds that came out of the clavier. They made him smile. But when he played two notes he didn't like, it made his ears hurt. He'd become so upset that he'd cry. Even as a tiny child, Wolfie knew which notes sounded right together and which notes did not.

Papa Leopold started giving Wolfie lessons, too. Soon Wolfie could play all the tunes in Nannerl's music notebook.

Keyboard Instruments in the 18th Century

Harpsichord

The harpsichord was the most popular of the early keyboard instruments. The strings were made of metal and plucked with quills. The metallic sound was not pleasing to musicians' ears, but Mozart figured out a way to make music sound more beautiful on the harpsichord.

Clavichord

The clavichord was basically a simpler and smaller version of harpsichord that people played at home.

Fortepiano

The name means "loud-soft." Its strings are struck by a covered hammer so the sound can be loud or soft. The fortepiano sounded much more pleasing to musicians and composers than the harpsichord. It also was the first instrument with levers that were worked by the feet. This, too, produced a richer sound.

Spinet

The spinet was a tabletop version of the harpsichord with fewer octaves and the same quality of sound.

Organ

The organ usually has two keyboards and pedals which play extra notes. Most music written for the organ is for church services. The huge sound is produced by air moving through pipes of different lengths.

As soon as Wolfie heard a tune, he could play it right back. Papa Leopold could hardly believe it. He made notes on how quickly and easily the little boy learned music.

Once, when Wolfie was about four, Papa Leopold saw a sheet of  "music" that the boy had been working on. At first, Papa laughed, thinking it was nonsense. But when he looked more closely, he realized that it was a musical composition. And a complicated one at that. Many of the notes were smudged and written over. He stopped laughing and asked Wolfie about it. Wolfie agreed that it was compli-cated. He said, "…you must practice until you can get it right…" and then he showed his father how it should be played.

At five, Wolfie composed two more pieces of music for the clavier. This means that he heard tunes in his head and played them. Amazed, Papa Leopold wrote them down in his notebook. Soon Wolfie was reading music. Papa Leopold saw that his son had a rare gift. He gave him special ruled sheets of music paper. That way, Wolfie could write down the music he heard in his head. Wolfie was writing music even before he learned to write words.

Years later, when Wolfie had grown up, his father wrote him a letter describing what he had been like: "As a child and a boy, you were serious rather than childish, and when you sat at the clavier or were otherwise intent on music, no one dared to have the slightest jest with you . . . your expression was so solemn."

Yet making music was also great fun for young Wolfie. He thought about it and played it all the time. Music was always part of the games that he invented. His father's friend, the musician Johann

Schachtner, came to live with the family for a while. He wrote, "If we, he and I, were carrying his toys from one room to another, the one of us who went empty-handed always had to sing or fiddle a

march as we went." Writing music let Wolfie express all his feelings. When he was happy, he would make up a fast tune, like an *allegro*. When he felt sad, he would make up a slow tune, called an *andante*. These are Italian words that composers and musicians use to describe how music should be played. When a piece of music should be played very slowly, it is called an *adagio*. If it should be played fast, it is a *presto*. Soft tunes, played lightly, are called *piano* or *pianissimo*. Loud tunes are labeled *forte* or *fortissimo*.

Like many children in the eighteenth century, Wolfie and Nannerl did not go to school. They spent the days in their small house where Papa Leopold was their only teacher—for music and everything else.

With Papa Leopold's help, Wolfie and Nannerl studied reading, writing, arithmetic, history, and geography. Later, when Wolfie started traveling, he learned foreign languages, like Italian and

French. (Wolfie and Nannerl grew up speaking German, as did everyone else in Austria.) He also studied the ancient language of Latin.

Papa was strict with lessons as he was with everything. Wolfie's mother, Anna Maria, was not as strict. Her father was a bass singer, so she knew about music. But although Mama sometimes tried to shield Wolfie and Nannerl from Papa's anger, she never openly went against him, either. Mostly, she agreed to what Leopold wanted.

One day, Leopold invited some musicians to his house. They were going to practice a piece of music that Leopold had written for the harpsi-chord and two violins. Wolfie, who was not quite seven, came into the room, holding a small, half-sized violin.

Parts of the Violin

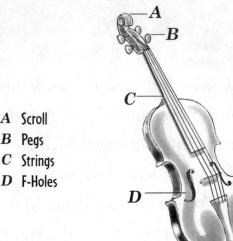

A Scroll
B Pegs
C Strings
D F-Holes

Papa Leopold had gotten the violin for Wolfie. But Papa hadn't started giving him lessons yet. Wolfie wanted to play with his father and his friends. But Papa Leopold said no. Wolfie had to wait until he learned how.

Wolfie began to cry.

One of the musicians was Papa's friend Johann Schachtner. He felt sorry for the little boy. He invited Wolfie to come play along side him. He told Leopold that if Wolfie played softly, no one would hear him play. That way, Wolfie would not disrupt the practice. Leopold agreed, but only if Wolfie promised to play very quietly. The musicians started playing. Herr Schachtner stopped playing after a few minutes. But Wolfie continued. Everyone was astonished. Wolfie had taught himself to play the violin. He also taught himself to play the organ.

Wolfie loved his father and wanted, more than anything, to please him. "Next to God comes Papa," he said. Every night before bed, he composed a different melody that he would sing out loud for Papa Leopold. Papa had to sing the second part of the melody. After the singing was done, Wolfie would kiss his father and go to sleep.

Although not as gifted as her brother, Nannerl was also a talented musician. She played the harpsichord. Encouraged by Wolfie, she composed music, too. Soon, news of Wolfie's and Nannerl's talents reached Vienna. Vienna was a big city and the capital of Austria.

One day, a messenger on a handsome white horse came to the Mozart home in Salzburg. Wolfie and Nannerl were asked to come to Vienna. There they would play before the Empress Maria Theresa.

It took the family nearly a week to get ready.

Finally, they boarded a stagecoach for Vienna. They had a lot of things to take with them. Besides their clothes, they packed a clavier, two violins, and cases of music. But they did not take Bumperl, their dog. He had to stay home.

The trip to Vienna took another whole week. The stagecoach moved slowly over the bumpy,

muddy roads. When it grew dark, the Mozart family stopped for the night at inns along the way. Finally, they arrived in Vienna.

The Hofburg Imperial Palace in Vienna

Vienna was a magical city, filled with palaces and castles. It was the home to the University. There were also many beautiful gardens and grand churches. Musicians came for its concert halls. Vienna was known as a center for music and art.

When Wolfie
was first introduced to
the empress, he ran right over and
jumped on her lap. Then he gave her a big hug
and lots of kisses. The empress, who was a mother

herself, was charmed. Later, when she heard Wolfie and Nannerl perform, she was deeply impressed by their playing.

At the palace, everyone dressed in the most splendid clothes. So the empress gave Wolfie and Nannerl each a special set of clothes to wear. Wolfie's new suit was lilac-colored and trimmed with wide, gold braiding. Wolfie liked the fancy clothes and wore them proudly. All his life, he would enjoy wearing beautiful and expensive outfits.

At one point during the visit, Wolfie tripped. He was helped up by the empress's daughter, Princess Marie Antoinette. Wolfie liked the pretty princess, who was seven. Right on the spot, he asked her to marry him. Everyone burst out laughing. Wolfie didn't understand that the little princess was already engaged to a French prince. One day, she would be the queen of France.

When the Mozarts returned home, Papa

Leopold and Mama had a lot of thinking to do. They realized that Wolfie and Nannerl were highly unusual children. Salzburg was not a big enough or important enough city for their talents. Leopold wanted the world to see—and hear—his exceptional children. Leopold decided he would take his children on a concert tour. They would perform for important people throughout Europe.

Leopold knew that they would be paid well for

If you're lucky enough to live near a museum with a collection of real 18th-century clothes, you can see the kind of fancy outfits Mozart wore. It's amazing to remember that these handsome clothes, usually embroidered, were made entirely by hand. The only tools available for sewing were scissors, needles, and a "goose"—an iron that could be heated over a fire.

Elegant men wore embroidered coats and vests and knee-length pants. Dresses for fashionable ladies were sometimes ridiculously fancy, with skirts that were six feet wide! A lady had to turn sideways to go through a door.

their work. Money was very important to Papa Leopold. He always worried about having enough. A long tour was just the thing to make the children famous—and the parents rich.

Empress Maria Theresa

Chapter 2
Seeing the World

In 1763, when Wolfie was seven years old, the Mozart family left Salzburg.

Setting out on a big sailboat, they glided down the Danube River. They went to the German cities of Stuttgart, Mannheim, Mainz, and Frankfurt. They also traveled by coach and visited other European cities like Brussels and Paris. A long trip like this was highly unusual, especially with children. Roads were bad, so getting anywhere took a long time. Traveling was also dangerous. Many times, thieves were on the roads, looking for people to ambush and rob.

Still, the Mozart family braved the dangers. In all the places they visited, Wolfie and Nannerl played for counts and countesses, dukes and duchesses, princes and princesses. Everyone wanted to hear them perform. Grownups were dazzled by the tiny children who played so well. Nannerl remarked in a letter on how the lords and ladies patted their arms and kissed them like puppy dogs.

On tour, Wolfie was often sick. Most days, he gave concerts in the early afternoon and evening. Sometimes he might give three concerts in a single day. He composed music in the morning and at night. Sometimes he stayed up all night and didn't go to sleep until dawn.

His parents saw that he was working too hard, and they hoped that rest was the cure. Wolfie did indeed overwork himself. But he may have also suffered from a kidney disease. The disease might have been what kept him from growing. He was always small for his age, and he remained short all of his life.

Because of the tour, the Mozart children grew more and more famous. Wolfie loved the compliments and the attention. He loved to be told how talented he was. He loved being hugged and kissed, even by strangers.

When the family arrived in a new city, Wolfie and Nannerl would play for the most important people in the local court. Then other rich people would hire them to play at parties. Payment was sometimes in money, other times in gifts. But sometimes the rich noblemen paid only a small amount of money. It was as if, Leopold complained, they thought their company was payment enough.

An artist named Lorenzoni was chosen to paint the children's portraits in 1763. Wolfie and Nannerl wore the beautiful clothing that the empress had given them. Because they had to stand still for so many hours, they became bored and restless. So Lorenzoni hired a trio of musicians

Johann Sebastian Bach

(1685-1750)

Born in Germany, Johann Sebastian Bach was a great musician and composer. His music influenced so many other musicians that he is called "the master of masters." He was the father of eleven sons—all of them were accomplished musicians. Although he did not live to meet Mozart, one of his sons did and became friends with Wolfie.

to entertain them. That made the time pass more quickly. Today, the portraits are in the Mozart Museum in Salzburg.

The Mozart family kept moving on. Their next stop was England. To reach London, they had to cross the English Channel. Unlike the calm Danube River, the Channel was dark, choppy, and wild. Wolfie and Nannerl were seasick from the motion of the boat going up and down over the waves. They were happy when they reached England.

While he was on tour, Wolfie did more than perform and compose. He also had a chance to meet famous musicians and composers of his day. In London, he met Johann Christian Bach, son of Johann Sebastian Bach. He loved discussing music with these people. When he talked about music, he didn't sound like a child, but like a mature man.

While the family was in London, Papa Leopold fell sick. He needed rest and quiet to get better, so

they left London and went to Chelsea, a village near the Thames River. For seven weeks, Wolfie and Nannerl could not practice their music because the noise might disturb Papa. Nine-year-old Wolfie needed something to do, so he composed a symphony—his first. It is called the Symphony in E-flat and is still performed today. Later Nannerl wrote, "I had to copy it out as I sat at his side. Whilst he composed and I copied, he said to me: 'Remind me to give the horn something worthwhile to do!'"

It is quite remarkable to think of a child writing a symphony. A symphony is a piece of classical music written for an orchestra, which, at that time, was made up of at least eight different instruments.

The 18th-Century Orchestra

The instruments that make up an orchestra have changed since Mozart's time. The way that they are grouped together has changed, too.

By the end of the 18th century, the harpsichord was no longer used. It was replaced by the fortepiano which could be played with much more depth and richness. The organ was not generally used in orchestras after this period, except for church music.

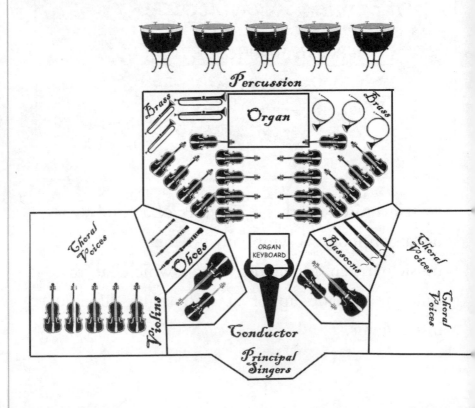

Orchestras always have at least eight instruments, one of which must be a violin. Musical instruments are divided into four types.

Percussion

Percussion instruments are instruments that are struck, such as the piano, the harpsichord, the clavier, drums, cymbals, and xylophone.

Strings

String instruments are played by vibrating strings. The violin, viola, violoncello, and bass viol are all string instruments.

Woodwinds

Woodwinds are played by blowing on a reed or across an opening. The flute, clarinet, oboe, English horn, saxophone, and bassoon are woodwinds.

Brass

Brass instruments such as the coronet, trumpet, French horn, trombone, and tuba are played by blowing into a circular mouthpiece.

A symphony lasts about thirty minutes and has three or four movements or sections. Some of the movements are slow and some are fast. Usually, the symphony begins with a fast movement, followed by a slow one. Then comes another lighter and faster one. If there is a fourth movement, it is even faster. Although the different movements are not alike, they are related to one another. Together they form a pleasing whole.

Papa Leopold recovered from his illness, but on the way back to Salzburg, Wolfie caught smallpox.

Soon, Nannerl came down with it, too. Smallpox was a highly contagious disease, something like chicken pox, only much more serious. Many people died from it. Wolfie and his sister lay in a darkened room, while their parents looked on anxiously. The doctor came and went. The days were long and filled with worry. Would the children get better?

Fortunately, both brother and sister did get well. The miracle boy was able to return home in 1766.

Although he was only ten years old, young Mozart was now an experienced, professional musician. He had met royalty and won their hearts with his playing and his own beautiful music. What would come next?

Chapter 3
The Wonder Boy Grows Up

Nine months after the Mozart family returned to Salzburg, Leopold and Wolfie were off again, back to Vienna. Wolfie was growing up. His father saw that he and Nannerl could no longer make a living as child geniuses. Nannerl was a good musician, but she would never be a great one. And while Wolfie was amazing for a young boy, when he became a man, his music might not seem so amazing. Then what would happen?

Papa decided Nannerl would

no longer go on concert trips. Instead, she would look for a husband to support her. (Eventually, Nannerl got married and had three children. Although she no longer performed, for the rest of her long life she continued to teach music.)

As for Wolfie, he needed to find a job as a concertmaster in the court of a king or prince.

During Wolfie's time, the only way to hear music was to hear it performed live. There were no CDs, tapes, or records. Kings and princes would hire musicians like Mozart to write and play music especially for them. In that way, they would always have beautiful music around them. And the musician, in turn, made a living by writing music and performing it.

Leopold also thought that it was time for Wolfie to make his debut as an opera composer. An opera is a story told entirely in songs and performed on a stage. Often an opera has ballet in it, too. Operas were very popular before there were

movies or television, because they told exciting, dramatic stories through music and dance. Many performers were involved: singers to sing the songs and act out the stories; musicians to play the music, dancers to perform the ballet. The performers wore gorgeous costumes, and the stage sets were beautifully painted and very elaborate.

Operas were performed in specially built opera houses in big cities like Milan, Paris, or Vienna. The opera houses themselves were grand places, with velvet-covered seats and fancy chandeliers. Altogether, an opera was a lavish spectacle enjoyed by the very rich who could afford the expensive tickets. An opera might take more than two hours to be sung; it usually had several acts, and there were intermissions between them.

Wolfie wrote his first opera before his thirteenth birthday. Although he composed several great operas later in life, his first attempt wasn't a success. The singers were angry at taking orders from a boy. They complained bitterly about the music and about Wolfie, too. The opera was canceled before it was ever performed. Wolfie did not receive the fee that had been promised to him.

Leopold was furious and thought that jealous composers were to blame. He wrote: "I can but tell you briefly that the whole hell of music is in revolt

to prevent the world from witnessing a child's cleverness. It is impossible for me to press for the performance of the opera, knowing that there is a conspiracy to spoil it . . . ."

But Leopold was not going to let this defeat his plans for Wolfie. From 1769 to 1773, Wolfie and his father made three trips to Italy, leaving his mother and Nannerl behind. Wolfie loved Italy, with its warm climate and golden light. He especially loved Venice, where people traveled in graceful boats, called gondolas, through water-filled streets called canals. These trips were an important part of Wolfie's musical education. In Italy, Wolfie was able to hear a different kind of

music. It was lighter and less serious than the music he was used to hearing and playing. This thrilled him. He loved learning about new kinds of music. He kept on composing, too, at a very rapid pace.

Much as he loved his new surroundings, Wolfie missed Mama and Nannerl. Letters filled in the gaps. "I kiss your hand a thousand times" and "I embrace my dearest sister with all my heart" he wrote home to them.

Leopold and Papa went to Rome during Holy Week, the seven days before Easter. Wolfie knew that a very famous piece of music called *Miserere* was going to be sung by the Pope's choir at St. Peter's Cathedral. That was the largest and most important Catholic

St. Peter's Cathedral

church. The *Miserere,* written by the composer Allegri, was very special and holy music. The music had never been printed. No one outside the Pope's choir had ever seen it. No other choir was allowed to sing it.

The service began. When Wolfie heard the glorious music filling the huge cathedral, he knelt down. He had never heard anything like it. Even when the service was over, he remained kneeling, as if in a trance. When Papa finally got him to

leave, he kept humming the music. He wanted to remember it always.

That night, Wolfie couldn't sleep. He kept hearing the music in his head. He got up and quietly searched for a pen and music paper. Then he sat down and began to write the notes he had heard. It all came back to him. Note for note, the great *Miserere* was down on paper. It was the first time this had ever been done outside the Pope's choir room. All his life, people would be astonished by Wolfie's ability to hear music and memorize it instantly.

From 1766, when he returned from his first

grand tour, to 1773, Wolfie wrote more than twenty symphonies, several string quartets, and three short operas, as well as concert songs and church music. He was only seventeen years old. Most musicians are just getting started at this age. But not Wolfgang. Although hardly more than a boy, he had written enough music for a lifetime.

Although music was his greatest "joy and passion," Wolfie found time to do other things. He enjoyed playing cards and billiards and writing to his family. He especially liked writing funny and silly letters to entertain and amuse his reader. They were filled with puns, jokes, and coded messages. To a cousin, he wrote, "Now, however, I do myself the honor of inquiring how you are and how you do. Have you good digestion? Have, you, perhaps, congestion? Can you tolerate me, do you think? Do you write with pencil or with ink?" Clearly, he was having fun by trying to make the words in his letter rhyme. He called Nannerl

Penmanship in the 18th Century

Beautiful handwriting was very important in the 18th century. People took pride in the look of letters and invitations. Pens were made from the tip, or quill, of the feather from a swan or turkey. Good writing paper was made from sheepskin. Letters were sealed by dripping hot wax on the paper, which was then stamped with a seal. The design of the seal could be a person's initials or coat of arms.

Penmanship was taught in school. The slope of the letters was supposed to be at a 54-degree angle. There were lots of other rules for writing properly, and it took many hours of practice to write in a graceful style, or "hand."

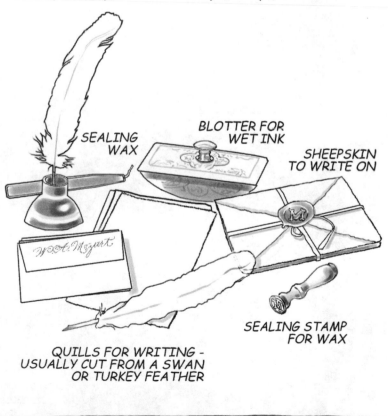

SEALING WAX

BLOTTER FOR WET INK

SHEEPSKIN TO WRITE ON

SEALING STAMP FOR WAX

QUILLS FOR WRITING - USUALLY CUT FROM A SWAN OR TURKEY FEATHER "horse face" in letters to her. He was playful and even silly, full of good spirits and affection for his family and friends.

When he was twenty-one, Wolfie fell in love with Aloysia Weber. She lived in Mannheim, Germany. Aloysia was the daughter of a musician as well as a musician herself. Wolfie wanted to marry her, but his father said no. Papa Leopold

told Wolfie to go to Paris, to "become famous and make money." Leopold's concerns about money and his family's future had only gotten stronger with the years. He insisted that Wolfgang help support the family.

At one point, Papa learned that Wolfie had stopped teaching some paying students because they hadn't shown up for a lesson. Instead, Wolfgang chose to teach others for free. That did not go over well with Leopold. Not at all. He scolded his son in an angry letter, saying, " . . . and you would rather, I suppose, leave your poor old father in need! The effort is too great for you, a young man, however good the pay, and it is more seemly, no doubt, that your fifty-eight-year-old father should run hither and thither for a wretched fee so that he may win the needful subsistence for himself and his daughter in the sweat of his brow . . . so that you, in the meantime, can amuse yourself giving a girl lessons for nothing!"

Bowing to his father's demands, Wolfie left Mannheim and Aloysia and went to Paris with his mother, although he continued writing letters to Aloysia. But his time in Paris was very disappointing. Wolfie was supposed to meet the Duchess

of Chabot. He hoped she would become his patroness. He would write his beautiful music for her, and in return, she would provide him with a steady living. But when he arrived at the mansion, the duchess rudely kept him waiting in an unheated, freezing outer room. At last, she asked him to join her guests, who were busy drawing. No one had the manners to stop drawing while he played on a clavier, so that Wolfie wrote how he made music for ". . . the sofas, the table and walls."

Also, Paris was so expensive. To make money, Wolfie began giving clavier lessons. But he didn't like the work. It meant less time to write his own music. And creating music was something he had to do. It was as necessary as eating or breathing. While in Paris, he did manage to compose a symphony. The symphony filled him with pleasure. The night before the premiere, he had heard the musicians rehearsing. How awful they sounded. They needed another rehearsal. But there was no time. He was so worried that the audience wouldn't

like the symphony that he planned to skip the concert. He went to bed "in a discontented and angry frame of mind."

The next day, however, Wolfgang changed his mind and went. To his surprise, the audience loved what they heard. They clapped and cheered. The Paris Symphony turned out to be a success after all.

Yet trouble soon followed.

His mother was not well. She suffered from earaches and sore throats. The chilly climate in Paris made her worse.  In her letters to Leopold, she complained of being cold all the time, even when there was a fire going in the room. In July of 1778, Anna Maria Mozart died.

Wolfgang was grief-stricken and stunned. His beloved mother was dead. How could he tell his father? Surely Leopold would somehow blame him. He wrote to a priest in Salzburg who was a family friend: "Mourn with me my friend!—This has been the saddest day of my life . . . I have to tell you that my mother, my dear mother is no more! . . . Let me now beg you to do me one friendly service, to prepare my poor father very gently for this sad news!"

When Leopold learned of his wife's death in a far-off country, he did indeed blame his son. He said that Wolfie had not only forced his mother to accompany him to Paris but also neglected her while they were there.

The way for Wolfgang to ease his sadness was to write music—often at a furious pace. It was how he dealt with his grief over his mother. In 1779, Wolfgang's father ordered him to come home. In Salzburg, Leopold had finally found a job for Wolfgang. Wolfgang was happy to leave Paris and its sad memories behind. Slowly and alone, Wolfie made his way back home.

Chapter 4
On His Own

Back in Salzburg, Wolfie became the court organist and concertmaster. He wrote music, at his usual fast pace. But he was bored. Then, in 1780, he was asked to compose an Italian opera for the court in Munich, Germany. Now this was exciting!

The Palace at Munich

Mozart loved opera and was eager to write one. And he could leave Salzburg again, where he was increasingly unhappy. His mother was dead. He and Nannerl, who was now a piano teacher, were no longer very close. Wolfgang longed to get away.

Mozart's opera was called *Idomeneo, King of Crete.* Like many operas, the story has a very complicated plot, based on an old legend. *Idomeneo* is about an ancient Greek king. After winning a long war against the Trojans, King Idomeneo is on his way home. Before the king's fleet of soldiers reaches shore, the ships are destroyed in a terrible storm. So Idomeneo makes a bargain with Neptune, god of the sea. If his own life is spared, he will sacrifice the first person he sees upon landing. That person turns out to be his very own son, Idamante. Horrified, Idomeneo breaks his promise to Neptune and tells his son to flee. This makes Neptune so furious that he creates a terrible sea monster.

Instead of running away, the king's son decides to fight the sea creature even though he thinks it means his own death. Miraculously he triumphs, and Neptune is no longer angry. With his father's and the sea god's blessings, the prince becomes the new king of Crete and marries a beautiful princess.

Idomeneo, King of Crete, was a

"Idomeneo, King of Crete"

big success. Leopold and Nannerl made the trip from Salzburg for the premiere. Wolfgang was happy with the enthusiastic reception to his work. Perhaps now he would be offered a permanent job in Munich. How much he would like that! Leopold and Nannerl could join him there. They would live together again.

But it was not to be. Soon after, Mozart was called to Vienna by Archbishop Colloredo, his old master from Salzburg. The relationship between the archbishop and the musician was stormy. The Archbishop did not appreciate Mozart. He was rude and insulting to him. He called Mozart a "knave," "scoundrel," "rascal," and "slovenly rogue." He even had Mozart kicked—in the seat of the pants—out of his house.

Mozart was angry and humiliated. Enough was enough. He decided to strike out on his own. This was a bold and risky thing for a musician to do. Without a rich patron, Mozart had no steady

salary. He would have to make his living from composing and giving concerts. What if he couldn't make enough money? How would he manage?

These same questions were on Leopold's mind when he heard what his son had done. How dare he leave such an important post! How irresponsible! Leopold was furious. But Mozart wouldn't budge. "My honor comes first with me, and I know that is the same with you," he wrote to his father. He

hoped his father would understand. But Leopold remained angry with his son, and continued to write him stern letters from Salzburg.

Soon, Leopold had another reason to be angry at Wolfie: Mozart had fallen in love again. Aloysia

Weber, his first love, no longer had any interest in him. Her younger sister, Constanze, however, was very taken with the talented composer.

Constanze was a singer and could appreciate Mozart's talents. But Leopold didn't care about all

Constanze Weber

that. In heated letters back and forth between father and son, Leopold told Wolfgang that he could not afford to marry. He said bad things about Constanze and her family. He accused the Webers of trying to trap Mozart into marriage.

Mozart still longed for his father's approval. He wanted Leopold to be happy for him. Wolfgang sent Leopold many gifts—a snuffbox, watch ribbons, a small crucifix decorated with a "little heart pierced by an arrow."

For Nannerl, there were some caps made by Constanze, "in the latest Viennese mode."

"Surely you cannot be vexed with me for wishing to marry?" he wrote home. "I implore you by all you hold dear in the world to give your consent to my marriage with my dear Constanze. . . . My heart is restless and my head confused; in such a condition how can one think and work to any good purpose?" Did Leopold consent to the marriage? No. He remained cold and disapproving.

But this time, Mozart went against his father's wishes. He was now in his twenties, and he was lonely. He loved Constanze and wanted her as his wife. In 1782, they married and set up housekeeping in Vienna. Mozart said farewell to Salzburg once and for all.

Chapter 5
Family Man

For the most part, Mozart and Constanze had a happy marriage. Often they struggled to make ends meet. There are stories about how the couple danced in their unheated house to keep warm and how they used their wooden furniture as firewood.

When Mozart ran out of money and could not pay his bills, he would teach, give concerts, and compose music at a frantic pace. He needed to make more and more money to keep up with his extravagant life. Often, he asked friends for a loan.

Even during the hard times, Constanze and Mozart loved each other and were glad to be together. Mozart described her as a woman with common sense and the kindest heart in the world. When they were apart, he wrote to her constantly, saying over and over how much he missed her.

Other times they had lots of money, but Mozart spent it as quickly as he made it. He bought fancy clothes and gave big parties with music, dancing, and lots of food. He even had his own coach, which cost a great deal of money.

Constanze and Wolfgang had six children, though only two sons, Karl Thomas and Franz Xaver, lived more than a year. Mozart taught his older son Karl Thomas to play the clavier and to sing. The whole family sang and played music together often. Sometimes, their pet bird, a starling, would join in the songs.

One day, Mozart received a visit from Franz Joseph Haydn. Haydn was twenty-four years older than Mozart. People thought he was the greatest living composer. After hearing Mozart play, he later told Leopold, "Your son is the greatest composer I know."

Mozart and Haydn became very close friends. Eventually, Mozart went on to compose many pieces of music that he dedicated to his "dear friend" Haydn. Some were piano concertos. These are pieces of music written for an orchestra with highlights for the piano. Others, eight in all, were for string quartets—two violins, a viola, and a bass.

Despite all the praise heaped on him, Mozart never became too proud. He valued his own music

but also appreciated the music of others. He knew that other composers had something to teach him. After hearing the music of Johann Sebastian Bach, he exclaimed, "Now here's something one can learn from!"

In 1787, Mozart became the chamber composer for Emperor Joseph II. This was a very important job—the most important one Mozart had ever held. He composed music and gave performances. The emperor paid his salary. At last he had a steady income.

Some of his greatest work dates from this time. *include*

In 1786, Mozart wrote *The Marriage of Figaro*, an opera that had beautiful music and yet was very funny. It tells the story of Figaro and Susanna, both servants to the Count and Countess. Figaro and Susanna are planning to marry. Meanwhile, the Countess is unhappy because her husband has been ignoring her. Susanna and Figaro think up

Vienna Opera House

a complicated plot to get the Count to pay attention to his wife. The plot involves disguises and false identities, but all ends happily.

The Marriage of Figaro opened at the Grand Opera House in Vienna and was a big success. The company went on

"*The Marriage of Figaro*"

to Prague, which was then part of Bohemia and is now in the Czech Republic. The opera was an even bigger hit there. Everywhere in Prague, people were humming the music from Mozart's opera or dancing to one of its lively tunes.

Mozart was thrilled by the reaction to his opera and wanted to thank the people of Prague. So he wrote a special symphony for them—the Prague Symphony—to express

Prague

his gratitude. But even more important, he was asked to write another opera. Written in 1787, the new opera, *Don Giovanni,* was not a comedy. It tells a much darker story, recounting the life and death of a wicked nobleman named Giovanni.

This opera, too, was a great success and brought Mozart more praise and fame.

In 1790, he wrote yet another popular opera. It was called *Così fan Tutte*, which, in English, means "everybody does it." The Italian poet Lorenzo Da

"Don Giovanni"

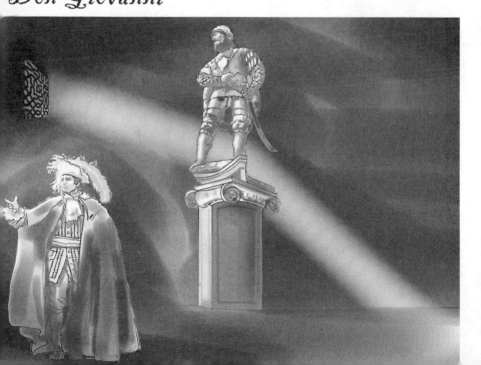

"Così Fan Tutte"
by W. A.
MOZART

Ponte wrote the opera's libretto—or the words—while Mozart composed the score. *Così fan Tutte* is another comic opera. It features a pair of officers, Ferrando and Guglielmo, and their sweethearts, Dorabella and Fiordiligi. The two young men want to test the love of the two women, and they invent many complicated tricks to do so. But all ends well for the two couples.

The last of Mozart's great operas, *The Magic Flute*, was written in 1791. Emanuel Schikaneder wrote the libretto. As its title suggests, *The Magic Flute* is like a fairytale: there is the evil Queen of the Night, her beautiful daughter, a handsome prince who loves her, wild animals, a set of chimes, and a golden flute. The prince faces many dangers, but in the opera's happy ending, he wins the hand of the princess. Once again, Mozart's hauntingly beautiful music enchanted all those who heard it.

"The Magic Flute"

Many people think that these operas are Mozart's finest works and that the years in Vienna were the most productive in his whole life. They were also probably the happiest years of his short life.

Chapter 6
An Untimely End

Despite the great popularity of his operas, Mozart still struggled to make enough money. The fickle members of the court and the nobility were always in search of something new. They began to lose interest in Mozart's work. His reputation suffered. He again had to ask his friends to lend him money. His father had died in 1787. Mozart brooded over the many quarrels they had when Leopold was alive. Mozart's own health was not good. He was often sick or in pain.

Yet despite all the troubles in his life, Mozart never stopped writing his exceptional music. He composed his last three symphonies in about three months. Unfortunately, he never had the chance to hear them played. It is amazing to think that he could hear all the different parts—strings, wood-winds, brass—in his head. He was so accurate that the music is performed today exactly as it was written. There were no corrections at all, because Mozart did not need to make them.

In July 1791, a very strange thing happened. Mozart was alone in his house. A stranger wearing

dark clothes and a dark hood came to the door. The stranger brought with him an unsigned letter. The letter asked Mozart to write a requiem. A requiem is a piece of music composed to honor a person who has died. The letter promised Mozart a lot of money for the job.

Who wanted the music written? And who was it for? Mozart did not know.

For the next several months, Mozart worked on the requiem. He thought about it all the time. His

health got worse and worse. Sometimes Mozart felt like he was writing the requiem for his own funeral. Soon he could not get out of bed. It became hard for him to breathe.

On December 4, 1791, he asked his friends to join him at his bedside. Together, they sang different parts of the requiem. On December 5,

Wolfgang Amadeus Mozart died. He was only thirty-five. The requiem remained unfinished, though the parts that he did complete are considered some of the most beautiful music he ever wrote.

His wife Constanze was grief-stricken when he died; she was also worried. What would happen to her and their children? A friend made the arrangements for Mozart's small funeral and burial in St.

Marx Cemetery, about three miles outside central Vienna. No stone or statue marked the spot where the great composer was buried.

After Mozart's death, Constanze married a man who became a loving stepfather to Karl Thomas and Franz Xaver. Although Mozart was gone, his music was not forgotten. And, in the end, that was what mattered most to Mozart. In 1842, a statue of Mozart was put up in Salzburg, his hometown. In 1856, one hundred years after Mozart had been born, there were big celebrations in Salzburg and Vienna. Karl Thomas, who was still alive, was there for the festivities in honor of his father.

Wolfgang Amadeus Mozart wrote more than 600 works. That is an astonishing number for any composer. It is even more astonishing when we think about how young he was when he died. Among these works were:

- 41 symphonies
- 27 piano concertos
- 5 violin concertos
- 27 concert arias
- 23 string quartets
- 18 Masses
- 22 operas

More than 200 years after he lived, people continue to play, listen to, and cherish Mozart's music. In 2002, on the one-year anniversary of the September 11 attacks, choirs around the world sang Mozart's requiem for a span of twenty-four hours in a global effort to honor those who died.

Although Mozart lived only a brief time, his music will live forever, bringing joy to listeners and musicians all over the world.

Timeline of Mozart's Life

1751	Wolfie's sister, Nannerl, is born
1756	Wolfgang Amadeus Mozart is born January 27, in Salzburg, Austria
1759	Wolfie learns to play the clavier at age three
1760	Wolfie composes his very first melodies
1762	Wolfie teaches himself to play the violin; Wolfie and Nannerl are invited to play for Empress Maria Theresa in Vienna
1763	Wolfie and Nannerl perform in Germany, Belgium, France, and England; the artist Lorenzoni paints the children's portraits
1765	Wolfie composes his first symphony, Symphony in E-flat, while in England
1768	Wolfie writes his first opera
1770	Mozart hears Allegri's *Miserere* at the St. Peter's Cathedral and writes it out from memory
1777	Mozart falls in love with Aloysia Weber
1778	Mozart writes the Paris Symphony; Mozart's mother Maria Anna dies
1780	Mozart is commissioned to write the opera *Idomeneo, King of Crete*
1782	Mozart marries Constanze Weber
1784	Mozart's son Karl Thomas is born
1786	*The Marriage of Figaro* opens at the Grand Opera House in Vienna
1787	Mozart composes *Don Giovanni*; Papa Leopold dies
1791	Mozart's son Franz Xaver is born; Mozart writes *The Magic Flute*; a mysterious stranger delivers a letter to Mozart commissioning a requiem; Mozart dies on December 5

Timeline of The World

French and Indian War begins	1754
Lisbon (Portugal) Earthquake kills 30,000 people	1755
The modern sandwich is created by the Fourth Earl of Sandwich	1762
John Hargreaves invents the spinning jenny, making it possible to weave raw fibers into thread faster than ever before	1764
Mapmaker John Spilsbury creates the first jigsaw puzzle	1767
James Watts patents the steam engine	1769
Marie Antoinette marries Louis XVI of France	1770
The first edition of Encyclopedia Britannica is published	1771
The waltz becomes a fashionable dance in Vienna	1773
American Revolution begins; Daniel Boone begins clearing the Wilderness Road into Kentucky	1775
James Cook discovers Hawaii	1778
Astronomer Frederick William Herschel discovers the planet Uranus	1781
The first successful hot-air balloon flight is recorded in Paris	1783
Benjamin Franklin invents bifocal glasses	1784
The Pennsylvania Quakers emancipate their slaves	1788
The French Revolution begins; George Washington is elected president of the United States	1789

BIBLIOGRAPHY

Brighton, Catherine. **Mozart: Scenes from the Childhood of the Great Composer.** Doubleday, New York, 1990.

Gay, Peter. **Mozart.** Viking, New York, 1999.

Isadora, Rachel. **Young Mozart.** Puffin Books, New York, 1997.

Mersmann, Hans, ed. **Letters of Wolfgang Amadeus Mozart.** Dover Books, New York, 1972.

Solomon, Maynard. **Mozart: A Life.** HarperCollins, New York, 1995.